WHAT GOLDENS TEACH US...

WHAT GOLDENS TEACH US...

LIFE'S LESSONS LEARNED FROM GOLDEN RETRIEVERS

© 2005 Willow Creek Press

Published by Willow Creek Press
P.O. Box 147, Minocqua, Wisconsin 54548

Editor/Design: Andrea Donner

Library of Congress Cataloging-in-Publication Data
Donner, Andrea K., 1967-
    What goldens teach us : life's lessons learned from golden retrievers / Andrea Donner.
          p. cm.
    ISBN 1-59543-150-0 (hardcover : alk. paper)
    1. Golden retriever--Miscellanea. 2. Golden retriever--Pictorial works. 3. Conduct of life. I. Title.
     SF429.G63D663 2005
     636.752'7--dc22

                              2004031056

Printed in Canada

Table of Contents

On
Healthy Living

Start
each day
with a smile.

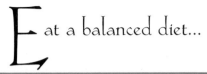

Eat a balanced diet...

But indulge yourself every now and then.

Try to avoid snacking between meals...

And if it doesn't fit in your mouth, don't eat it!

And remember, everything in moderation...

Or be prepared to pay the consequences.

Get a thorough check-up every year...

And plenty of exercise every day.

Keep well groomed to look and feel great.

© Norvia Behling

Drink
plenty of
liquids throughout
the day.

Yoga...

And meditation are great for relaxation.

Never turn down a belly rub.

Scratch what itches.

$\mathbb{C}$ atch a few winks whenever you can.

K eep a
positive
attitude.

On
Getting Along
with Others

I's good to
know that a
friend's got
your back.

Engage in
PDAs (public
displays of
affection)
with the ones
you love.

Don't believe every bit of gossip you hear.

Everything is more fun when shared with a friend.

A simple hug can make the difference between a good day and a not-so-good day.

Make
eye contact
if you want
something.

Kindness is one of the greatest gifts
you can give to the young.

B eing with somebody you love makes you feel like you're on top of the world.

There's nothing quite like a hug and a kiss.

Make sure to plan activities around the family.

Be patient with children's whims.

Don't squabble over petty things.

Be the kind of friend that others can lean on.

Be open to unexpected friendships.

Always support a friend in need.

Appreciate the companionship of your friends.

Play more.

Worry less.

It sure feels good to get a word of praise now and then.

Everyone likes to be complimented.

Being helpful to others always feels good.

Stick up for your friends.

On Self-Esteem
&
Self-Improvement

Respect the earth — recycle when possible and don't litter.

Make the most of your potential...

And utilize to the utmost your innate
strengths and natural abilities.

Be happy with who you are.

Never stop exploring.

Lead, don't follow.

Savor
the joyful
moments in
your life.

$\int$ peak up if you have something to say.

You can't hide from your problems...

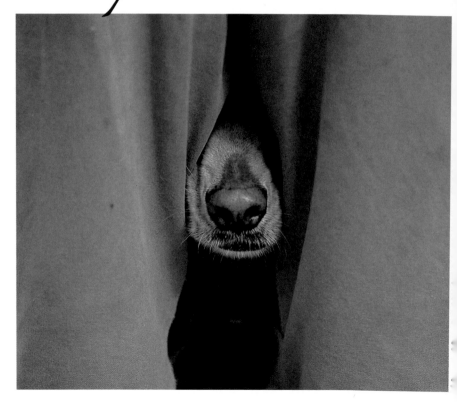

Y ou have to force yourself to go out and face them.

I f the world seems like too much on some days, take time out to care for and protect yourself...

A better day always comes around.

We can attain great things with guidance and encouragement.

Push your-
self to try
difficult and
challenging
things.

K eep a healthy sense of curiosity.

K eep up on current events.

But don't get buried under the bad news of the day.

If you find yourself in a hole
that's getting too deep...

S top digging.

Be proud of your abilities...

But don't
become a
showoff.

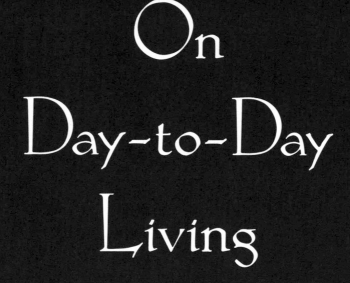

On
Day-to-Day
Living

$\mathbb{B}$e wary of strangers until
you can size them up.

Look forward to someone you love coming home.

The best time for a quick nap is right now.

Don't snoop.

Don't be afraid to look foolish now and then.

E veryone feels lonely sometimes...

But if you look, a friend can always be found.

Y ou won't find happi- ness on the other side of the fence.

The chase is often better than the catch.

Live life in the moment — surf the wave.

Be grateful for the small things in life.

Do your fair share of the household chores...

And be as helpful as you can.

Don't hold a grudge.

Be a friendly neighbor.

Cherish every gift, no matter how small.

Be proud
of your
heritage.

O
n
some days,
act your shoe
size instead
of your age.

A smile cheers up everyone's day.

Always make time to appreciate
this beautiful world.